Wedding Words

A Bride's Guide to Marriage Services

Rev. Alan Northcott

www.Florida-Beach-Wedding.net

Copyright Notice

Alan Northcott
924 S Easy Street, Sebastian, FL 32958
        www.Florida-Beach-Wedding.net

This publication is designed to provide accurate and authoritative information in regard to the subject matter covered. It is sold the understanding that the publisher is not engaged in rendering legal, accounting, or other professional services. If legal advice or other expert assistance is required, the services of a competent professional person should be sought.

First Printing, 2015

ISBN-13: 978-1508420088

ISBN-10: 1508420084

Printed in the United States of America

Contents

CHAPTER TWELVE: SAMPLE CEREMONY 75

Foreword

If you are like many people, you are looking for something unique on your wedding day. That's probably why you picked up this book. It is a special day, the memories of which should last a lifetime, and you do not want it to be like anybody else's.

The challenge, if you decide that you do not want a conventional marriage in a church of your religion, is to come up with the most meaningful ceremony that you can, combining the sanctity of the occasion with those personal touches that make it your own.

As a minister, I have performed weddings on the beach, on mountaintops, and in people's backyards. Each was special to the participants and a personal statement. This book is designed to help you express yourself in what may be the most significant day of your life.

I have collected together many different forms of ceremony, broken down into the functional sections that make up the complete occasion. Some elements are common to virtually every marriage, and some such as a butterfly release only occur occasionally. The intention of setting them out in this book is that you will be able to select the words that appeal to your heart.

Of course, there are many different ways of saying the same thing, and you may find that the contents are merely a starting point for you to create a custom service for yourself. Nevertheless, combining the different sections will provide you with a workable outline, and it is up to you whether you decide to do further customization.

In doing this, rest assured that the actual requirements for you to be legally married are minimal, and allow you great flexibility in your choice. Your selected minister will know what applies in your state, but generally, all you have to do is obtain a marriage license and have a ceremony where you confirm your intent to be married. In some states, as for example in Florida where I live, you do not even need to have witnesses sign the certificate, although many people do.

For some, "Dearly Beloved" in the opening words is the single strongest indicator that a marriage is about to take place; others prefer a more casual beginning. The selection of service sections I have included in this book takes that into account. Please read and be inspired to create the perfect day for yourself.

Rev. Alan Northcott

http://www.Florida-Beach-Wedding.net/

4 | Wedding Words

Chapter One:
How To Use This Book

This is a book about the ceremony of marriage. It is designed to help those participating in a wedding to find the right words to suit the occasion, and therefore may be principally of use to the bride and groom who want to design their own special wedding. It could also be incorporated in a wedding officiant's library for inspiration in their work.

Each chapter of the book gives you a choice of passages for a particular part of the service, along with commentary to help you choose. While you may wish to read through them all, many of them are not necessary and not used in every service. The notes will tell you which ones are optional and which constitute a conventional wedding.

Having said that, when you are considering your own wedding and not using an established conventional religious service, you are reasonably free to choose whatever words you wish. In fact, doing that makes it the most memorable day for you. So if you want to, you can use this book simply as an aide-memoire to remind you what passages you would like to include and go ahead and craft your own sentences.

Above all, remember it is your day and you are free to make it as special as you like. And if you have any other ideas for interesting additions, and would like to share them, then send them to me at alannorthcott@MSN.com and I will see if I can include them in future editions.

I have used Name#1 to represent the Groom's name and Name#2 for the Bride's name in the following text.

Chapter Two:
Greeting

The greeting is when the ceremony starts, after the bride and groom have approached the minister. You will always want to have some form of announcement to indicate that the wedding is underway. If it hasn't been done before, the minister should first remind people to silence their electronic devices - I used to request they be turned off, but that is impossible nowadays when so many people use them for pictures and video.

Often the greeting is used by the minister to summarize the importance of the day, and call everyone's attention to what is about to take place.

Greeting 1

Dearly beloved: we have come together in the presence of God to witness and bless the joining together of this man and this woman in holy matrimony. The bond and covenant of marriage were established by God in creation, and our Lord Jesus Christ adorned this manner of life by his presence and first miracle at a wedding in Cana of Galilee. It signifies to us the mystery of the union between Christ and his church, and Holy Scripture commends it to be honored among all people.

The union of husband and wife in heart, body, and mind is intended by God for their mutual joy; for the help and comfort given one another in prosperity and adversity; {and, when it is God's will, for the procreation of children and their nurture in the knowledge and love of the Lord}. Therefore marriage is not to be entered into unadvisedly or lightly, but reverently, deliberately, and in accordance with the purposes for which it was instituted by God.

Into this holy union Name#1 and Name#2 now come to be joined. If any of you can show just cause why they may not lawfully be married, speak now; or else forever hold your peace.

Greeting 2

Dearly beloved, we are gathered together here in the sight of God and the presence of these witnesses to join together this man and this woman in holy matrimony. Marriage is an honorable estate, instituted by God at the time of creation for the well-being of humankind. It is safeguarded by the laws of Moses, affirmed by the words of the prophets, and hallowed by the teachings of our Lord Jesus Christ. Marriage is a close and enduring union, a relationship in which a man and a woman forsake all others to become one flesh. This abiding union illustrates the holy relationship between Christ and his church. Marriage is therefore not to be entered into by any lightly, but reverently, soberly, and in the fear of God.

Greeting 3

I would like to welcome you to this joyful occasion of the marriage of Name#1 and Name#2. We are present here to recognize the beauty of their love and their intention to be together from now until the end of time. They are committing themselves to love, share, trust, and grow with another person, and we are witness to their beginning a whole new life with each other.

Greeting 4

Friends, we are gathered here today to witness the marriage of Name#1 and Name#2. Let us call upon God to be with us today as we celebrate this union of two into one. In the name of the Father, the Son and the Holy Spirit.

Chapter Three:
Opening Prayer

The Opening Prayer allows you to call on a higher power, usually known as God though some people may prefer other names such as the Supreme Being. It creates a pause and reverence for what is to follow, and validates the wedding with your personal beliefs.

Prayer 1

Let us pray.

Oh Lord of life and love, of light and faith, who in Jesus Christ our Lord gave your blessing at the wedding in Cana of Galilee, be present here this day as these two come to be joined as wife and husband. Even as they have been drawn together in love for each other, now join them in a love born out of their desire to walk in your path.

Amen

Prayer 2

Let us pray.

Father, hear our prayers for Name#1 and Name#2, who today are united in marriage before your altar. Give them your blessing, and strengthen their love for each other as each day passes. We ask this through our Lord Jesus Christ, your Son, who lives and reigns with you and the Holy Ghost, one God forever and ever.

Amen

Prayer 3

Let us pray.

Eternal God, our Creator and Redeemer, be present here this day as these two come to be joined as wife and husband. Look with favor on Name#1 and Name#2 and pour out your richest blessings on them as they stand before us in your presence, ready to assume the privileges and responsibilities of a Christian marriage. May you guide them step-by-step from this day forth as they begin their journey together as husband and wife. We ask this in the name of your son, Jesus Christ.

Amen

Prayer 4

Let us pray.

Almighty God, hear our prayers for Name#1 and Name#2 who have come here today to be united in the sacrament of marriage. Increase their faith in you and in each other, and through them bless your church. Make their love fruitful so that they may be living witnesses to your divine love in the world. We ask this through our Lord Jesus Christ, your Son, who lives and reigns with you and the Holy Spirit, one God, forever and ever.

Amen

Prayer 5

Let us pray.

Almighty and ever living power, we gather here in your presence to witness the commitment of these two people to one another. Grant that they will hold dear to their faith in you, and be with them as they travel through their life's journey together.

Amen

Chapter Four:
The Charge

The charge or declaration of intent is a precursor to the vows. It is traditionally a reminder of the seriousness of the occasion, and what the bride and groom are committing themselves to. Once they have listened to this, there can be no doubt that they should realize that they are taking the biggest step of their lives.

Charge 1

You have come here today to pledge your love before God and before the Church here present in the person of the Priest, your family and friends.

In becoming husband and wife, you give yourselves to each other for life. You promise to be true and faithful, to support and cherish each other until death, so that your years together will be the living out in love of the pledge you now make.

May your love for each other reflect the enduring love of Christ for his Church.

As you face the future together, keep in mind that the Sacrament of marriage unites you with Christ, and brings you, through the years, the grace and blessing of God our Father. Marriage is from God; He alone can give you the happiness which goes beyond human expectation, and which grows deeper through the difficulties and struggles of life.

Charge 2

Name#1 and Name#2, as you stand here, I remind you of the serious nature of the step that you are about to take. Marriage is a full commitment of two people to each other, and you are today declaring your intent to love each other for a lifetime.

There will be challenges along the way, and it is only with an earnest and sincere heart that you may be sure of your continued happiness and growth together.

Charge 3

Name#1 and Name#2, I charge you both as you stand in the presence of God to remember that covenant love alone will prevail as the foundation of a happy and enduring home. Let Christ, who was loyal to his own unto death, be your example. Let the apostle Paul be your teacher, who wrote: "Love is patient and kind; love is not jealous or boastful; it is not arrogant or rude. Love does not insist on its own way; it is not irritable or resentful; it does not rejoice at wrong, but rejoices in the right. Love bears all things, believes all things, hopes all things, endures all things." If you keep this steadfast love ever before you and, remaining faithful to each other, resolutely endeavor to fulfill the vows you now will make, God's blessing will be upon you, and the home you establish will endure through life's every change.

Charge 4

I require and charge you both, here in the presence of God, that if either of you know any reason that you may not be joined in holy matrimony lawfully and in accordance with God's word, you do now confess it.

.

Chapter Five:
Who Gives . . . ?

Traditionally, the bride's father used to "give away" the bride at a wedding ceremony. As such, this may be seen as a sexist ritual of more relevance in a chauvinistic society. Despite this, for many it is another traditional part of the service, which marks it as a true wedding ceremony.

Sometimes the inherent sexual bias of this act is circumvented by having each family participate in a blessing or commitment in support of the marriage, so this version too is included in this chapter.

Father

Who gives this woman to be married to this man?

The bride's father comes forward, says, *"I do"*, and places the bride's right hand in the groom's hand. He may then step back and be seated.

Family 1

This day Name#1 and Name#2 leave their parents to establish a new home as husband and wife. Therefore I would ask the parents of both Name#1 and Name#2 to give their blessing to this marriage.

Do you, Mr. and Mrs. (Parents of groom) give your blessing to them, and promise them your continued love and support?

We do

Do you, Mr. and Mrs. (Parents of bride) give your blessing to them, and promise them your continued love and support?

We do

Family 2

God's intention is that we leave our parents to be joined to our husband or wife. This is why when parents give their daughter away, they are endorsing a biblical principle in this assent. They are agreeing that as mother and father, they are no longer the primary people in their daughter's life, and they are giving their blessing to the marriage. This also applies to the groom's parents.

With that in mind, who gives this woman to be married to this man?

Mother and father: *We do*
Do the parents of the groom likewise give him to be married to this woman?

Mother and father: *We do*
(To both parents) *Will you support them with your love, and help them to grow together as a new family unit, under Christ our Lord?*
All parents: *We will*

Chapter Six:
The Consent

The consent is the precursor to the vows. It establishes once and for all that the bride and groom are free and unencumbered of any other relationships, and are willing to take the final step of vowing their lives to each other.

Consent 1

To the groom:

Name#1, will you have Name#2 to be your wife, to live with her, respect her, and love her as God intends with the promise of faithfulness, tenderness, and helpfulness, as long as you both shall live?

Response:

I will, with God's help.

To the bride:

Name#2, will you have Name#1 to be your husband, to live with him, respect him, and love him as God intends with the promise of faithfulness, tenderness, and helpfulness, as long as you both shall live?

Response:

I will, with God's help.

Consent 2

Name#2, will you have this man to be your husband; to live together in the holy estate of matrimony? Will you love him, comfort him, honor and keep him, in sickness and in health; and, forsaking all others, be faithful unto him as long as you both shall live?

I will.

Name#1, will you have this woman to be your wife; to live together in the holy estate of matrimony? Will you love her, comfort her, honor and keep her, in sickness and in health; and, forsaking all others, be faithful unto her as long as you both shall live?

I will.

Consent 3

Name#1 and Name#2, you have come together here today so that the Lord may seal and strengthen your love in the presence of the Church's minister and this community of your family and friends. In this way you will be strengthened to keep mutual and lasting faith with each other and to carry out the duties of marriage. And so, in the presence of the church and this community of your family and friends, I ask you to state your intentions.

Name#1 and Name#2, have you come here freely and without reservation to give yourselves to each other in marriage?

(Both) *We have.*

Will you love and honor each other as husband and wife for the rest of your lives?

(Both) *We will.*

Will you accept children lovingly from God and bring them up according to the Law of Love and Compassion?

(Both) *We will.*

Since it is your intention to enter into marriage, you have declared your consent before God and his Church, and this community of your family and friends.

Consent 4

Name#1, will you have Name#2 to be your wedded wife, to live together in the holy estate of matrimony? Will you love her, comfort her, honor and keep her, in sickness and in health; and forsaking all others, keep yourself only for her so long as you both shall live?

I will

Name#2, will you have Name#1 to be your wedded husband, to live together in the holy estate of matrimony? Will you love him, comfort him, honor and keep him, in sickness and in health; and forsaking all others, keep yourself only for him so long as you both shall live?

I will

Chapter Seven:
Sand, Candles, Wine . . .

Many couples are deciding to add something extra to their marriage ceremony by incorporating an additional element. In this section we look at the sand ceremony, where the bride and groom mix together sand which can never then be separated; the candle ceremony, where both bride and groom come together to light one candle from two separate candles, signifying their unification; and the wine ceremony, where the bride and groom sip from the common cup.

None of these actions is a necessary element for a wedding, but frequently they will be added to make the day more memorable.

In a later section, we have butterfly and dove releases, bubbles, and cord braiding. Those elements are better positioned towards the end of the ceremony.

Sand

Use two glass containers of different colored sands, and pour into an empty glass container.

And now, Name#1 and Name#2. Each container of sand represents each of you, and as the sands are poured together, they will be joined together as one. Just as these grains of sand can never be separated once poured, so will your marriage be, united as one for all the days of your life.

Candle1

For the candle ceremony, the bride and groom each need a lit candle. They can light these themselves from an altar candle, or sometimes the mothers will take part in this ceremony (the Best Man may assist) and hand the lit candles to their offspring. In addition, there is an unlit Unity Candle, best positioned towards the congregation. As the bride and groom light the Unity Candle together, the minister says: –

The Unity Candle serves as both a symbol of the combining of two separate lives into one, and as a sign of God's light and presence. Therefore, I would encourage you on each anniversary to light this candle and remember this day, recalling the promises made by you and God's promise to dispel darkness and be present with you in your marriage always.

Candle 2

With similar actions to Candle 1, here is a more profound statement of the significance: –

As you light your separate candles, we remember and honor your uniqueness and separate being until this day. The candle represents the light of your being, the special gifts and talents and all that makes you who you are as an individual.

When you light the third candle, you celebrate the power of the separate flames to ignite a common flame of passion and commitment as you come together as one. The dancing flame symbolizes the beauty and vitality of your love for each other, which will enrich and sustain you in the years that lie ahead.

Wine

As with the candle ceremony, the actions of the Wine Ceremony are followed by the minister offering words on the symbolism. Often, the minister will hand a glass of wine to the groom who takes a sip, then offers it on to his bride. After she sips, the glass is handed back to the minister.

As an alternative, you could have a glass each and drink them with linked arms. There is more risk of spillage with this technique, so you might at least want to avoid red wine, even though it is more visually attractive than white.

Wine is a symbol of life, like the blood that flows through our veins. As you both share this loving cup today, two become one, your paths intertwined, each separate, but united in love.

May this cup serve as a loving cup for your relationship. Fill it with forgiveness, understanding, and appreciation, and be sure to drink deeply and frequently from it.

Chapter Eight:
Vows, Promises & Rings

The vow is a necessary part of the ceremony, expressing the actual commitment to the marriage. It can be taken in various ways. Often the bride and groom will repeat the words after the minister says them, and this is perhaps the most familiar form.

An alternative which has grown in popularity is for the bride and groom to each write their own vows, and thus to state them independently of the minister. This can be the most embarrassing, nerve-racking, yet rewarding part of the ceremony, fraught with danger but able to bring the strongest to tears. As a practical matter, no matter how well you may think you have memorized the words, you should be sure to bring a written version with you for support. You may even ask the minister to hold a copy and provide prompting if necessary.

If all this appears too difficult, as an alternative you can have the minister read out the vows and simply confirm your assent.

Rings are included in this chapter, as sometimes the vows will include the exchange of rings. Alternatively, the rings may be presented immediately after the main vows.

Vows 1

Groom repeats after the minister.

I, Name#1, take you, Name#2, to be my wedded wife, to have and to hold, from this day forward, for better for worse, for richer for poorer, in joy and in sorrow, in sickness and in health, to love and to cherish till death us do part, and thereto I pledge you my troth.

Bride repeats after the minister.

I, Name#2, take you, Name#1, to be my wedded husband, to have and to hold, from this day forward, for better for worse, for richer for poorer, in joy and in sorrow, in sickness and in health, to love and to cherish to death us do part, and thereto I pledge you my troth.

Vows 2

Do you, Name#1, take Name#2 to be your wife? Do you promise to be true to her in good times and in bad, in sickness and in health? Will you love her and honor her all the days of your life?

I do.

Do you, Name#2, take Name#1, to be your husband? Do you promise to be true to him in good times and in bad, in sickness and in health? Will you love him and honor him all the days of your life?

I do.

Rings 1

Almighty God, bless these rings, symbols of faithfulness and unbroken love. May Name#1 and Name#2 always be true to each other, may they be one in heart and mind, may they be united in love forever, through Christ our Lord.

Amen.

Groom repeats after the minister.

Name#2, wear this ring as a sign of our faithful love. In the name of the Father, and of the Son and of the Holy Spirit.

Bride repeats after the minister.

Name#1, wear this ring as a sign of our faithful love. In the name of the Father, and of the Son and of the Holy Spirit.

Rings 2

Lord, bless and consecrate Name#2 and Name#1 in their love and compassion for each other. May these rings be a symbol of the true faith they share in each other and always remind them of their love and compassion. We ask this through Christ our Lord.

The groom places the ring on the bride's finger. He repeats after the minister.

Name#2, take this ring as a sign of my love and fidelity. (In the name of the Father and the Son and the Holy Spirit.)

The bride places the ring on the groom's finger. She repeats after the minister.

Name#1, take this ring as a sign of my love and fidelity. (In the name of the Father and the Son and the Holy Spirit.)

Rings 3

Bless, O Lord, these rings to be a sign of the vows by which this man and this woman have bound themselves to each other; through Jesus Christ our Lord.

Amen.

Name#1 repeats after minister:

Name#2, I give you this ring as a symbol of my vow, and with all that I am, and all that I have, I honor you, in the name of the Father, and of the Son, and of the Holy Spirit.

Name#2 repeats after minister:

Name#1, I give you this ring as a symbol of my vow, and with all that I am, and all that I have, I honor you, in the name of the Father, and of the Son, and of the Holy Spirit.

Chapter Nine:
Blessing/Benediction

After all the commitments are made, it is common to have a prayer or blessing before the final pronouncement. This section does not last long, but sets a seal on the ceremony.

Blessing 1

Eternal God, maker of all and source of all life and peace, we pray that Name#1 and Name#2 may now be blessed in their relationship by your holy presence. Grant they may be forgiving to each other when they make mistakes; grant them wisdom and devotion that each may be to the other a strength in need, a comfort in sorrow, and a companion in joy; and that they may grow in love and peace with you and with one another all the days of their lives.

Amen

Blessing 2

Let us ask God to bless Name#2 and Name#1, now married in Christ, and unite them in his love.

God, our Father, creator of the universe, you made man and woman in your own likeness, and blessed their union. We humbly pray to you for this bride and groom today united in the sacrament of marriage. May your blessing come upon them. May they find happiness in their love for each other and enrich the life of the Church.

May they praise you in their days of happiness and turn to you in times of sorrow. May they know the joy of your help in their work and the strength of your presence in their need. May they worship you with the Church and be witnesses in the world. May old age come to them in the company of their friends and may they reach at last the kingdom of heaven.

We ask this through Christ our Lord. Amen

Blessing 3

Let us pray to the Lord for Name#2 and Name#1 that they may always be united in love for each other.

Holy Father, you created humankind in your own image and made man and woman to be joined as husband and wife in union of body and heart, so fulfilling their mission in this world.

Lord, grant that as they begin to live this sacrament they may share with each other the gifts of your love and become one in heart and mind as witnesses to your presence in their marriage. Help them to create a home together (and give them children to be formed by the gospel and to have a place in your family).

Give your blessing to Name#2, your daughter, so that she may be a good wife (and mother), caring for the home, faithful in love for her husband, generous and kind.

Give your blessing to Name#1, your son, so that he may be a good husband (and *father), caring for the home, faithful in love for his wife, generous and kind.*

We ask this through Christ our Lord.

Amen.

Blessing 4

My dear friends, let us turn to the Lord and pray that he will bless with his grace this woman Name#2 now married in Christ to this man Name#1 and that he will unite in love the couple he has joined in this holy bond.

Father, by your plan man and woman are united, and married life has been established as the one blessing that was not forfeited by original sin or washed away in the flood.

Look with love upon this woman, your daughter, now joined to her husband in marriage. She asks your blessing. Give her the grace of love and peace. May she always follow the example of the holy women whose praises are sung in the scriptures.

May her husband put his trust in her and recognize that she is his equal and the heir with him to the life of grace. May he always honor her and love her as Christ loves his bride, the Church.

Father, keep them always true to your commandments. Keep them faithful in marriage and let them be living examples of Christian life. Give them the strength which comes from the gospel so that they may be witnesses of Christ to others. (Bless them with children and help them be good parents. May they live to see their children's children.) And, after a happy old age, grant them fullness of life with the saints in the kingdom of heaven. We ask this through Christ our Lord.

Amen.

Blessing 5

Let us pray.

O Eternal God, Creator and preserver of all humankind, giver of all spiritual grace, the author of everlasting life, send your blessing on this man and this woman whom we bless in your name; that they, living faithfully together, may surely perform and keep the vow and covenant made between them, and may ever remain in perfect love and peace together, and live according to your laws through Jesus Christ our Lord.

Amen.

Benediction

Go forth into the world in peace. Be of good courage. Hold fast to that which is good. Render to no one evil for evil. Strengthen the fainthearted, support the weak, help the afflicted, show honor to all. Love and serve the Lord, rejoicing in the power of the Holy Spirit. And the blessing of God Almighty, the Father, the Son, and the Holy Spirit, be upon you and remain with you forever.

Amen.

Chapter Ten:
Butterflies, Doves,
Bubbles and Braids

As mentioned previously, it is best to delay butterflies, doves, and bubbles until near the end of the ceremony. As you can imagine, once these are released, they not only bring joy and happiness, but also serve to disrupt the proceedings, which therefore should be virtually over.

Butterflies

Butterflies are one of the more risky features, in my opinion. They will come with detailed instructions, which basically say that they should remain in a refrigerated condition until a certain number of hours before the ceremony. This way, they are quiescent until needed.

Assuming all goes well, they will wake up in time to flutter away when the box is opened. They may need some encouragement, and you will find that some, once released, decide to hang around and make even settle in the aisle. These are all things that you will have to deal with; however, it is beautiful to see their fluttering as they slowly leave the area, and in this they score over a dove release which is quickly finished with.

Butterflies are as beautiful as they are fragile. By their transformation from a caterpillar, they symbolize the way that true love transforms the lives of two people. As you have been joined today in marriage, your commitment to love releases into the world a new beauty and perfection. May your love transform itself and everyone it touches into its most beautiful form.

Doves

A dove release is another way to make your wedding memorable. Once again, this is best done as the final act of the ceremony. I must admit I'm always concerned with what happens to the creatures that we release into a strange environment, and wonder how they will find their bearings. Nonetheless, this is a graceful conclusion to the marriage ceremony.

Doves are beautiful creatures. Watching them soar together is inspiring and a joy.

Let these doves symbolize your love, devotion, peace, and loyalty. As you release them, let them take your hopes and dreams up into the heavens, from whence they will come back to you.

Bubbles

I have not taken part in a Bubble Blessing, but imagine it can be the most delightful occasion. I believe it is best if bubbles are handed out to the guests when they arrive, so they may all take part.

Name#1 and Name#2 would like you all to open up your bubbles, and participate in this joyous moment. Please join with me in wishing their relationship will flourish and grow through their long and happy lives together, and in blowing your bubbles out to the Universe, send with them your wishes and prayers for the blessed union that we are celebrating today.

Please take a deep breath now, and send your blessings with the bubbles into this beautiful day.

Cord braiding

Today, Name#2 and Name#1 have chosen to braid three strands together into a single cord. Each strand has a significant meaning. The gold strand represents God and His majesty. The purple strand represents the groom and his life. The white strand represents the bride and her life.

In braiding these three strands together, Name#2 and Name#1 have demonstrated that their marriage is more than a joining of two lives together. It is a unity with God as well. They have chosen to allow God to be at the center of their marriage, woven into every aspect of it.

As Ecclesiastes 4:9-12 reads, "Two are better than one, because they have a good return for their work: If one falls down, his friend can help him up. But pity the man who falls and has no one to help him up! Also, if two lie down together, they will keep warm. But how can one keep warm alone? "Though one *may be overpowered, two can defend themselves. A cord of three strands is not quickly broken."*

Chapter Eleven: Pronouncement/ Presentation

The announcement finalizes the wedding ceremony, and the presentation that follows formally introduces the couple as a couple to the community of friends. The pronouncement is usually followed by the first married kiss, before the celebrant sends the couple off down the aisle.

You may want to think about the style of address. Do you want to have both first names included, or simply "Mr. & Mrs. Name#1 LastName . . . ."?

Pronouncement 1

Name#1 and Name#2, you have chosen to come here today to be joined in holy wedlock. You have exchanged your vows before God and these witnesses, and have declared your commitment to each other by exchanging rings.

I now pronounce in Jesus name that you are husband and wife together, in the name of the Father, and of the Son, and of the Holy Spirit. Those whom the God has joined together, let no one put asunder.

You may now kiss the bride.

Pronouncement 2

For as much as Name#1 and Name#2 have consented together in holy wedlock and have witnessed the same before God in this company and have pledged their faith to each other and have declared the same by joining hands and by giving and receiving rings, therefore, by the authority granted to me as a minister of Jesus Christ, I pronounce that they are husband and wife together, in the Name of the Father, and of the Son, and of the Holy Spirit. Those whom God has joined together, let no one put asunder.

You may now kiss the bride!

Pronouncement 3

Name#1 and Name#2, you have exchanged your vows and made your promises, and have marked your union with the giving and receiving of rings.

It is therefore now my pleasure to pronounce you husband and wife. You may seal this union with a kiss.

Presentation 1

And now, to all the friends and family here present who have come to celebrate this marriage, it is my great pleasure to present, for the first time anywhere, Mr. & Mrs. . .

Presentation 2

Now it is my pleasure to present, for the first time anywhere, Mr. and Mrs. . .

Chapter Twelve:
Sample Ceremony

I hope you have been inspired by these words to determine what direction you want your ceremony to take. You can make it as formal or as casual as you wish, and you can incorporate your own quirks to make it a more special day.

Some prefer to stick with the more traditional and expected format. Here as an example is a wedding that I officiated at, which was largely traditional but had the simple addition of a braiding ceremony.

-O-

Opening Words

Dearly beloved, we are gathered together here in the sight of God and the presence of these witnesses to join together this man and this woman in holy matrimony. Marriage is an honorable estate, instituted by God at the time of creation for the well-being of humankind it is safeguarded by the laws of Moses, affirmed by the words of the prophets, and hallowed by the teachings of our Lord Jesus Christ. Marriage is a close and enduring union, a relationship in which a man and a woman forsake all others to become one flesh. This abiding union illustrates the holy relationship between Christ and his church. Marriage is therefore not to be entered into by any lightly, but reverently, soberly, and in the fear of God.

Charge to Couple

Name#1 and Name#2, I charge you both as you stand in the presence of God to remember that covenant love alone will prevail as the foundation of a happy and enduring home. Let Christ, who was loyal to his own unto death, be your example. Let the apostle Paul be your teacher, who wrote: "Love is patient and kind; love is not jealous or boastful; it is not arrogant or rude. Love does not insist on its own way; it is not irritable or resentful; it does not rejoice at wrong, but rejoices in the right. Love bears all things, believes all things, hopes all things, endures all things." If you keep this steadfast love ever before you and, remaining faithful to each other, resolutely endeavor to fulfill the vows you now will make, God's blessing will be upon you, and the home you establish will endure through life's every change.

Consents

Name#1, will you have Name#2 to be your wedded wife, to live together in the holy estate of matrimony? Will you love her, comfort her, honor and keep her, in sickness and in health; and forsaking all others, keep yourself only for her so long as you both shall live?

I will

Name#2, will you have Name#1 to be your wedded husband, to live together in the holy estate of matrimony? Will you love him, comfort him, honor and keep him, in sickness and in health; and forsaking all others, keep yourself only for him so long as you both shall live?

I will

Who gives this woman to be married to this man?

I do

Vows

(Name#1 takes Name#2's hand and repeats:)

I, Name#1, take you, Name#2, to be my wedded wife, to have and to hold, from this day forward, in plenty and in want, in joy and in sorrow, in sickness and in health, to love and to cherish to death us do part, and thereto I pledge you my troth.

(Name#2 takes Name#1's hand and repeats:)

I, Name#2, take you, Name#1, to be my wedded husband, to have and to hold, from this day forward, in plenty and in want, in joy and in sorrow, in sickness and in health, to love and to cherish to death us do part, and thereto I pledge you my troth.

Rings

Bless, O Lord, these rings to be a sign of the vows by which this man and this woman have bound themselves to each other; through Jesus Christ our Lord. Amen.

(Name#1 repeats after me:)

Name#2, I give you this ring as a symbol of my vow, and with all that I am, and all that I have, I honor you, in the name of the Father, and of the Son, and of the Holy Spirit.

(Name#2 repeats after me:)

Name#1, I give you this ring as a symbol of my vow, and with all that I am, and all that I have, I honor you, in the name of the Father, and of the Son, and of the Holy Spirit.

Three Cords of Unity

Today, Name#2 and Name#1 have chosen to braid three strands together into a single cord. Each strand has a significant meaning. The gold strand represents God and His majesty. The purple strand represents the groom and his life. The white strand represents the bride and her life.

In braiding these three strands together, Name#2 and Name#1 have demonstrated that their marriage is more than a joining of two lives together. It is a unity with God as well. They have chosen to allow God to be at the center of their marriage, woven into every aspect of it.

As Ecclesiastes 4:9-12 reads, "Two are better than one, because they have a good return for their work: If one falls down, his friend can help him up. But pity the man who falls and has no one to help him up! Also, if two lie down together, they will keep warm. But how can one keep warm alone? "Though one may be overpowered, two can defend themselves. A cord of three strands is not quickly broken."

Blessing

Let us pray.

O Eternal God, Creator and preserver of all humankind, giver of all spiritual grace, the author of everlasting life, send your blessing on this man and this woman whom we bless in your name; that they, living faithfully together, may surely perform and keep the vow and covenant made between them, and may ever remain in perfect love and peace together, and live according to your laws through Jesus Christ our Lord.

Amen.

Pronouncement

For as much as Name#1 and Name#2 have consented together in holy wedlock and have witnessed the same before God in this company and have pledged their faith to each other and have declared the same by joining hands and by giving and receiving rings, therefore, by the authority granted to me as a minister of Jesus Christ, I pronounce that they are husband and wife together, in the Name of the Father, and of the Son, and of the Holy Spirit. Those whom God has joined together, let no one put asunder.

You may now kiss the bride!

The Benediction.

Go forth into the world in peace. Be of good courage. Hold fast to that which is good. Render to no one evil for evil. Strengthen the fainthearted, support the weak, help the afflicted, show honor to all. Love and serve the Lord, rejoicing in the power of the Holy Spirit. And the blessing of God Almighty, the Father, the Son, and the Holy Spirit, be upon you and remain with you forever. Amen.

Now it is my pleasure to present, for the first time anywhere, Mr. and Mrs. . . .

About the Author

I have been ordained for about 10 years, and it is one of the highest privileges to be able to perform a wedding ceremony for a couple in love. As a minister, I have a responsibility for a key part of the wedding day, though I appreciate that there are many other parts that demand much more diligence and attention to ensure that they proceed smoothly.

In officiating in a wedding, a pastor participates in one of the most momentous happenings of life, and it is a sacred experience. My faith background is Christian, though I am open to other forms of belief and non-belief, with the overriding principle of respect for an individual's choice.

If you have any questions or comments on this book, or if I can be of service for your wedding, I would love to hear from you. Just e-mail me at alannorthcott@msn.com.